# SATAN'S SECRET PYLON

# 𝖘𝖆𝖙𝖆𝖓'𝖘 𝖘𝖊𝖈𝖗𝖊𝖙 𝖕𝖞𝖑𝖔𝖓

*An exposition of the Satanic philosophy*
*at the heart of the*
**Apostolic Johannite Church**

By

Mgr. +Reginald Freeman, Ep. Gn., I.L., DD
Former Executive Director of the
Friary / Ordo Sacrae Flammae

## Tri▲dPress
Fox Lake, IL

**Satan's Secret Pylon**: An exposition of the Satanic philosophy at the heart of the Apostolic Johannite Church

By Reginald Freeman

ISBN-13: 978-1-946814-17-3

Triad Press, LLC
123 S. US 12 #33
Fox Lake, IL 60020

# Disclaimer

This work is a theological and philosophical analysis intended for scholarly and initiatic audiences. It presents the author's interpretations, critiques, and comparative research regarding the doctrines, rituals, and internal structures of the Apostolic Johannite Church (AJC), the Friary / Ordo Sacrae Flammae (OSF), and related bodies.

Where claims of doctrinal borrowing or textual replication are made, they are supported by cited documents and direct comparisons. These observations are offered not as personal accusations, but as contributions to the ongoing discourse surrounding transparency, lineage, and spiritual integrity within modern esoteric organizations.

The author affirms respect for the freedom of belief and practice, and does not seek to defame individuals or institutions. Readers are encouraged to engage critically and form their own conclusions based on the evidence presented.

# Contents

# Preamble

Let me begin with clarity: while recent events have contributed to the timing of this monograph, the ideas and concerns it addresses have occupied my thoughts for many years. This is not a personal attack, nor a reactionary defense. It is the result of long-standing theological reflection, initiatic experience, and comparative analysis.

I do not make a habit of publicly questioning the doctrines or practices of any church or religious philosophy. However, the persistent discrepancies between public statements and private teachings within the Apostolic Johannite Church (AJC) and its initiatic counterpart, the Friary / Ordo Sacrae Flammae (OSF), warrant careful scrutiny. These discrepancies are not merely historical curiosities—they touch upon the integrity of spiritual transmission and the legitimacy of doctrinal claims.

My reasons for writing this work are not rooted in personal grievance, though I acknowledge that recent defamatory attacks—cloaked in the language of moral concern—have underscored the urgency of transparency. My past misdeeds are a matter of public record, and I have taken full responsibility for them. The thesis presented here, however, stands on its own merits, independently of those

1

events. It is a product of years of initiatic engagement, doctrinal study, and comparative research across esoteric traditions.

What follows is not a polemic, but a call for doctrinal honesty and spiritual accountability. I offer this work to fellow seekers, initiates, and scholars—not as final judgment, but as contribution. May it provoke thought, inspire dialogue, and serve the greater work of illumination.

Accountability, responsibility, and transparency are good things. They are necessary for mental health and spiritual growth. To avoid accountability, to actively seek to repress the truth, is to plant a cancerous seed that will ultimately blossom into a psychovorous monstrosity. I am therefore going to do for my brethren in Christ at the AJC the great favor of helping them to take the first steps toward their own accountability.

There are statements published by the AJC concerning their history and doctrine – statements that have been circulated for many years – that are manifestly inaccurate; to such a degree that one might even consider them "deceptive" and "disingenuous" – or even "dangerous." It is imperative, therefore, for the health of the AJC and that of its hierarchy who actively conceal dark truths, that the cleansing power of daylight be shed upon these facts at long last.

Due to my own former experience and activity within the AJC and its auxiliary body, the Ordo Sacrae Flammae (Friary) – acting as co-consecrator of the current Patriarch of the AJC (Mar Iohannes IV) to the episcopate, and serving as the first Executive Director of the Friary/OSF under the nomen mysticum of Magister Dositheus – I certainly have ample personal recollections that I could share regarding the early days of this organization; not to mention my former close personal and working relationship with the current Primate of the AJC for the United States (Mar Thomas), who served as my first episcopal consecrator, and whom I personally initiated as Martinist S.I. and I.L. But so as not to subject my revelations to dismissal as hearsay or slander, I will try to confine my statements to what can be verified empirically. The documentary evidence I have is vast and incontrovertible. My archives include documents, photographs, and a/v recordings that reveal much more even than I intend to address in this format. It will not take much to illustrate my principal points.

Before proceeding, I want to make clear that the following facts are not at all intended to embarrass or reflect poorly upon the many women and men of good faith who participate in AJC activities innocently and with every wholesome intention. Nevertheless, it is important to know what and whom you are supporting – including the foundational doctrine of your church. Likewise, I place no judgment on the doctrine itself. The Gnostic community, since antiquity, has been an arena of diverse theological and doctrinal ideas. It is only the attempt at concealment that I wish to address here. It is my hope that these disclosures may help the leadership of the AJC find the transparency, accountability, and frankness that they aver to so ardently seek.


Mgr. +Reginald Freeman, Ep. Gn., I.L., DD
Sunday, September 14, 2025
Feast of the Exaltation of the Holy Cross

# Foundations

Let us begin our investigation with the statements issued by the AJC and made available on their public website. In order to get a clear understanding of where the AJC is today, and why they think and act in the manner they do, we must go back to the very origins of the church. In their FAQ, they pose the question: "I read somewhere your Church was founded by a Satanist. Is that true?" Their response is as follows:

> This is sometimes raised as a way of discrediting the AJC.
>
> It is true that our founder some time prior to establishing the Church, was a member of a so-called "left-hand path" (rather than Satanist) organisation as a part of his spiritual journey. As he stated at the time, feeling that this path seemed to provide more opportunity for personality conflicts than genuine spiritual growth and drawn by a growing interest in Gnostic Christianity, he made a firm break with that period of his life. He had no involvement with that organisation or path by the time he founded the church.
>
> For more information on this and other attacks please see the letter from the Patriarch.

Is this statement truthful, or is it a lie? There are five components to which we can look when attempting to discern a lie: Blaming, Minimizing, Rationalizing, Self-Deception, and Avoidance. So, let's examine at this statement, one part at a time, and see if we can determine its truthfulness.

> *This is sometimes raised as a way of discrediting the AJC.*

There is really not much to comment upon here. On its face, the attempt to discredit a Gnostic church by crying "Satanism" is practically a time-honored tradition among fundamentalists and so-called orthodoxy. And if such accusations were made in absence of any evidence, as is often the case, it would not be worth addressing in the least. Unfortunately, the smoke billowing forth from this accusation has its source in the Black Flame of the Temple of Set. As you will come to see, given the evidence that is to be laid out, what we have here is not merely a flat denial. Rather, it is the beginning of Blaming and Minimizing.

> *It is true that our founder some time prior to establishing the Church, was a member of a so-called "left-hand path" (rather than Satanist) organisation as a part of his spiritual journey.*

Here we see Minimizing in full effect. This body to which they are referring is none other than the Temple of Set. To identify the Temple of Set as "a so-called 'left-hand path' (rather than Satanist) organisation" goes far beyond mere Minimizing, and into the realms of Rationalization, Avoidance, and certainly Self-deception if they actually believe what they are peddling. While the ToS may not emphasize the character of Satan in the way some other Satanic organizations do, they are a direct offshoot from the Church of Satan, their required study materials include the *Satanic Bible* and several other Satanic texts, and every impartial analysis of the body recognizes it as part of the Satanic current. And how do we know that this "left-hand path" organization is the Temple of Set? I know this, of course, from first-hand knowledge. But as I stated previously, I am going to rely on documentary evidence. And we will get to this incontestable evidence a little further on.

> *As he stated at the time, feeling that this path seemed to provide more opportunity for personality conflicts than genuine spiritual growth and drawn by a growing interest in Gnostic Christianity, he made a firm break with that period of his life.*

As this statement is made about the founder rather than by him, I will limit my criticisms. Let me just state that all evidence suggests that rather than making a "firm break with that period of his life," all evidence points instead to a seamless transition from the Temple of Set to the Apostolic Johannite Church; preserving intact every crucial point of philosophical doctrine. That is to say, the evidence that we will furnish shortly will show that whether Setian or Gnostic, these labels are merely façades masking an underlying philosophy as developed by the Temple of Set.

*He had no involvement with that organisation or path by the time he founded the church.*

The statement that he "had no involvement" with the organization of the Temple of Set at the time of the founding of the AJC may or may not be true. But to state that he had no involvement with the "path" is an outright fabrication, as will be shown convincingly. Herein we have the summation of the lie.

*For more information on this and other attacks please see the letter from the Patriarch.*

By all means. Let's look at the letter. Though, rather than shedding more light on these accusations of Satanism, they instead dig a deeper hole of deceit. The relevant passages:

1. Alleged Satanism: Some time prior to establishing the Church, our founder had examined the "Left Hand Path" as a part of his spiritual journey and practice through membership in the "Temple of Set". Feeling that this path did not provide an opportunity for genuine spiritual growth and drawn by a growing interest in Gnostic Christianity, he made a firm break with that period of his life. He had no involvement with that path or organization by the time he founded the church, nor did any of the beliefs, values or rituals of the associated path or organization form the basis of the Apostolic Johannite Church.

The Apostolic Johannite Church has never been, is not now, nor will ever be Satanic, nor for that matter is it associated with any organizations of a left-hand path or Satanic character. Nor are our clergy involved in any Satanic rituals.

First, credit where credit is due. Rather than using mitigating terms such as "so-called" and "rather than Satanist," this statement comes right out and names the Temple of Set. But let us highlight some of the additional information given here, so that we may refer back to it in our examination of the inner doctrine of the AJC and its initiatic counterpart, the OSF/Friary.

> *...nor did any of the beliefs, values or rituals of the associated path or organization form the basis of the Apostolic Johannite Church.*

I dislike sounding repetitive, but again, this is simply untrue. Actually, it is more than simply untrue, it is the diametric opposite of the truth. What makes statements such as this so diabolical, is that it is not the simple whitewashing of an inconvenient historical fact, it is the deliberate perversion of the truth for the purpose of concealing and misleading.

> *The Apostolic Johannite Church has never been, is not now, nor will ever be Satanic, nor for that matter is it associated with any organizations of a left-hand path or Satanic character.*

We have here again a doubling down of the lie. Not only is it associated with left-hand path organizations, *it is itself a left-hand path* organization masquerading as Gnostic Christian.

> *Nor are our clergy involved in any Satanic rituals.*

Ummm...I'm going to leave this one alone for now. To address this may require an additional monograph.

In summary, we have shown already certain falsehoods and deceptions contained within their denial of Satanic activity. In the next sections we will get into the meat of it. That is to say, we will examine certain documents and analyze certain of their contents to show an undeniable Setian/Satanic/left-hand path structure and philosophy that comprises the inner teachings of this church.

## Organizational Attributes

Firstly, we need to identify the real connection between the AJC and the Friary/OSF. The AJC website attempts to make an arbitrary distinction, stating:

> The two organisations are distinct and membership in one does not require membership in the other...

This may be technically true, but it is misleading. The Friary has always served as the "inner order" of the AJC. The fact that, as stated on the AJC website, "the leadership of the Friary is always invested in a Bishop of the AJC," illustrates, I think, the absolutely integral relationship between the bodies. And unsurprisingly, it is this secret, inner conclave composed of the hierarchy of AJC clergy, that establishes and instructs the egregore of the movement as a whole. It is then the lower initiates, or those outside of the Friary proper, but participating in the rites of the AJC, that feed this egregore. This is basic occult physics.

Before we get to the actual doctrine of the Friary, we'll look at one of the organizational documents: the By-laws. We will compare them, side by side, with the corresponding by-laws of the Temple of Set.

| By-Laws of the OSF *(2002)* | By Laws of the ToS *(1999)* |
|---|---|
| Article 1. Offices | ARTICLE 1. Offices |
| Section 1.01 | Section 1.01. |
| The principal office for the transaction of the business of this Friary is located in the City of Cincinnati, Ohio, United States of America. | The principal office for the transaction of the business of this corporation is located in the City and County of San Francisco, California, United States of America. |
| Section 1.02 | Section 1.02. |
| The Friary may also have offices at such other places, within or without the State of Ohio where it is qualified to do business, as its business may require and as the Grand Master may from time to time designate. | The corporation may also have offices at such other places, within or without the State of California where it is qualified to do business, as its business may require and as the High Priest may from time to time designate. |

| | |
|---|---|
| Article 2. Affiliation | ARTICLE 2. Affiliation |
| Section 2.01 | Section 2.02. |
| An individual member of the Friary may be a member of, or affiliated with another initiatory organization or institution. | An individual member of the Temple of Set may be a member of, or affiliated with another primarily religious organization or institution during I° membership status only. |
| Article 3. Membership | ARTICLE 3. Membership |
| Section 3.01 | Section 3.01. |
| There shall be five degrees of membership in the Friary: Friar I°, Friar Adeptus Minor II°, Friar Adeptus Major III°, Magister, or Magistra Templi IV°, Grand Master V°. | There shall be six degrees of membership in the Temple of Set: Setian I°, Adept II°, Priest or Priestess of Set III°, Magister or Magistra Templi IV°, Magus or Maga V°, and Ipsissimus or I |
| Section 3.02 | Section 3.02. |
| Any person may become an Initiate I° who has attained the age of eighteen (18) years, is in sympathy with the purposes of the Friary, has indicated an interest in furthering its program, and has found a current II°+ member willing to admit them via the appropriate Initiation Rite. | Any person may become a Setian I° who has attained the age of eighteen (18) years, is in sympathy with the purposes of the Temple of Set, has indicated an interest in furthering its program, has contributed to the Temple of Set the admission fee, and is admitted to membership by a member holding the III°+... |

13

Section 3.03

An Initiate may be Recognized to Friar Adeptus Minor II° by any current III°+ member willing to confer upon them the appropriate Initiation Rite.

Section 3.04

A Friar Adeptus Minor II° may be Recognized to Friar Adeptus Major III° by any current IV°+ member willing to confer upon them the appropriate Initiation Rite.

Section 3.05

A Friar Adeptus Major III° may be Recognized to Magister or Magistra Templi IV° by decision of the College of Seven, the corporate board of Directors for the Friary.

Section 3.06

The I° and II° constitute the Outer Order or Lesser Mysteries.

Section 3.07

The III° and IV° constitute the Inner Order or Greater Mysteries.

Section 3.08

The name Friary is generally applied to the

Section 3.03.

A Setian may be Recognized to Adept II° if a member holding the III°+ deems that person deserving of the II°...

Section 3.04.

An Adept may be Recognized to Priest or Priestess of Set III° if a member holding the IV°+ deems that person Elect to the III°.

Section 3.05.

A Priest or Priestess of Set may be Recognized to Magister or Magistra Templi IV° by decision of the High Priest.

entire Order, but properly refers only to the Outer Order; the name of the Inner Order is Ordo Sacrae Flammae.

Section 3.09

Persons holding the I° or II° may be expelled from the Friary by a member of the College of Seven. Such a decision must be communicated in writing to the Grand Master and to the Dean of the College of Seven within ten days following the decision.

The decision to expel a member should never be made lightly, and may be overturned by a simple majority vote of the College of Seven.

Section 3.10

Persons holding the III° may be expelled from the Friary only by decision of the Grand Master, ratified by a simple majority vote of the College.

Section 3.08.

Persons holding the I° or II° may be downgraded in degree and/or expelled from the Temple of Set by a member holding the III°+. Such a decision must be communicated in writing to the High Priest and to the Executive Director voluntarily.

Section 3.09.

Persons holding the III° may not be involuntarily downgraded in degree. They may be expelled from the Temple of Set by decision of the High Priest. Such a decision must be communicated in writing to the Executive Director and to all voting Councillors within fifteen days following that decision, and at least five persons who are voting Councillors must indicate their approval of

the decision in writing to
the High Priest and
Executive Director.

Section 3.11

Persons holding the IV°
may be expelled from the
Friary by decision of the
Grand Master, ratified by a
unanimous vote of the
College of Seven.

This section may not be
invoked to expel an
incumbent Member of the
College

Section 3.10.

Persons holding the IV°
may not be involuntarily
downgraded in degree.
They may be expelled from
the Temple of Set by
decision of the High Priest.
Such a decision must be
communicated in writing to
the Executive Director and
to all voting Councillors
within fifteen days
following that decision, and
at least six persons who are
voting Councillors must
indicate their approval of
the decision in writing to
the High Priest and
Executive Director. This
section may not be invoked
to expel an incumbent
Councillor or an
incumbent Executive
Director.

Section 3.12

Only members of the
College of Seven shall be
considered voting members
of the Friary for purposes
of amending these By-Laws.

Section 3.14.

Only persons who hold the
III°+ shall be considered
voting members of the
Temple of Set for purposes
of amending these By-Laws.

Section 3.13

The names and addresses
of all members of the
Friary shall be made

Section 3.15.

The names and addresses
of all members of the
Temple of Set shall be

16

available to any member of the College upon demand.

made available to any III°+ member upon demand.

## Section 3.14

Any member of the Friary may withdraw from the Friary by notifying the Grand Master, Dean of the College, or any member of the College in writing.

## Section 3.18.

Any member of the Temple of Set may withdraw from the Temple of Set by so notifying any III°+ member in writing. The III°+ member must then communicate the withdrawal to the Executive Director in writing.

## Section 3.15

Readmission of any former member of the Friary who was not involuntarily dismissed from the Friary for misconduct shall be at the discretion of any II°+ member of the Friary. Any individual so readmitted does so at the I° level.

## Section 3.20.

Readmission of any former member of the Temple of Set who was not involuntarily dismissed from the Temple for misconduct shall be at the discretion of any III°+ member of the Temple. Any individual so readmitted must comply with any procedures determined to bring membership status current as determined by the Executive Director.

## Section 3.16

Readmission of any former member of the Friary who was involuntarily dismissed from the Friary for misconduct shall be at the discretion of the Grand Master. Such a readmission

## Section 3.21.

Readmission of any former member of the Temple of Set who was involuntarily dismissed from the Temple for misconduct shall be at the discretion of the High Priest. Such a readmission authorized by the Grand Master must be communicated in writing to the Dean of the College of Seven, and all Members of the College, and at least three voting Members of the College must indicate their approval of the decision in writing to the Grand Master and Dean.

Article 4. College of Seven

Section 4.01

The Board of Directors of the Friary shall be known as the College of Seven. All references to "the College" in these By-Laws refer to the College of Seven.

Section 4.02

The College of Seven shall consist of seven persons, each of whom holds the IV°. In addition to these seven persons, the Grand Master shall be an ex officio member of the College, serving without vote.

Section 4.03

Each voting Member of the College shall serve "ad vitam."

Section 4.04

authorized by the High Priest must be communicated in writing to the Executive Director and all Councillors, and at least five voting Councillors must indicate their approval of the decision in writing to the High Priest and Executive Director.

ARTICLE 4. Council of Nine

Section 4.01.

The Board of Directors of the Temple of Set, Inc. shall be known as the Council of Nine. All references to "the Council" in these By-Laws refer to the Council of Nine.

Section 4.02.

The Council of Nine shall consist of nine persons, each of whom holds the III°+. In addition to these nine persons, the High Priest and the Executive Director shall be ex officio members of the Council, serving without vote.

These College members have a conjoint responsibility to uphold the By-Laws and to assist the Grand Master to govern the Order justly, for and on behalf of the members, in the Light of the Sacred Flame. This responsibility has spiritual as well as temporal connotations and shall take precedence over, but shall not replace their individual duties.

Section 4.05

The Dean of the College of Seven makes all appointments to the College from among current members holding the IV°. Only the Grand Master may remove a sitting member of the College of Seven.

Section 4.06

Incapacity of a Member of the College to execute his office shall be determined by the Dean of the College. Such a determination must be approved in writing by a minimum of four other voting members of the College, such approval to be communicated to the Grand Master and the Dean of the College.

Section 4.05.

Permanent incapacity of a Councillor to execute his office shall be determined by the Chairman of the Council. Such a determination must be approved in writing by a minimum of six other voting members of the Council, such approval to be communicated to the High Priest, the Chairman

of the Council, and the
Executive Director.

Section 4.07

The Grand Master and the
Dean of the College of
Seven will ensure that the
assets of the Friary, both
administrative and
financial, are used to the
greatest reasonable extent
to assist the College in
carrying out its activity.

Section 4.08

As soon as possible
whenever the office of Dean
of the College of Seven
becomes vacant, the Grand
Master shall appoint a new
Dean from among a sitting
member of the College of
Seven.

The first action of the new
Dean must be to appoint a
IV° member to replace the
vacancy caused by his
appointment.

Section 4.07.

The High Priest and the
Executive Director will
ensure that the assets of the
Temple of Set, both
administrative and
financial, are used to the
greatest reasonable extent
to assist the Council in
carrying out its activity.

Section 4.08.

As soon as possible
following July 1 and not
later than August 1 of each
year, the High Priest shall
appoint one of the voting
members of the Council of
Nine to serve as Chairman
of the Council of Nine,
term of office to expire
August 31 of the following
year or upon the
confirmation of the next
Chairman. Such an
appointment must be
approved in writing by at
least six persons who are
voting members of the
Council, such approval to
be communicated to the
High Priest and the
Executive Director. The
incumbent Chairman of
the Council shall serve as

Chairman until the election of the successor.

Section 4.09

If the Friary finds itself concurrently with no Grand Master or Dean, then the voting member of the College with the longest current continuous membership on the College will serve as Grand Master. The first action of the new Grand Master must be to appoint a IV° member as Dean of the College of Seven.

Section 4.10

All Members of the College shall serve without compensation.

Section 4.10.

All Councillors shall serve without compensation. They shall be reimbursed for reasonable expenses involved in carrying out the functions of their office. Determination of reasonable expenses shall be made by the Chairman of the Council.

Article 5. Dean of the College of Seven

Section 5.01

The Dean shall perform all duties of a corporate Board Chairman required by law.

Section 5.02

The Dean shall hold the IV°.

Section 5.03

Upon appointment to office, the Dean shall serve "ad vitam" until his resignation or removal from office. He may resign from office by so notifying both the Grand Master and the College of Seven in writing.

Section 5.04

The Dean of the College of Seven may be recalled by a unanimous vote of the remaining six

members of the College.

Section 5.05

The Dean of the College of Seven serves without compensation.

| | |
|---|---|
| Article 6. Grand Master | ARTICLE 5. High Priest of Set |
| Section 6.01 | Section 5.01. |
| The responsibility and authority to determine all policies and programs of the Friary, subject only to | The responsibility and authority to determine all policies and programs of the Temple of Set, subject |

the provisions of these By-Laws, shall rest with the Grand Master. No policy, program, decision, action, or statement under the authority of this Section shall conflict in whole or part with the By-Laws of the Friary.

only to the provisions of these By-Laws, shall rest with the High Priest (or High Priestess) of Set. No policy, program, decision, action, or statement under the authority of this Section shall conflict in whole or part with the Articles of Incorporation or By-Laws of the Temple of Set.

Section 6.02

The Grand Master shall perform all duties of a corporate president required by law.

Section 5.02.

The High Priest shall perform all duties of a corporate president required by law.

Section 6.03

The Grand Master shall hold the honorary V°.

Section 5.03.

The High Priest shall hold the IV°+.

Section 6.04

The Grand Master must also hold the position of Bishop, or Bishop-Elect in the Apostolic Johannite Church. If Bishop-Elect, the Grand Master must be consecrated to the Episcopacy in the Apostolic Johannite Church within six months of his appointment.

Section 6.05

Upon appointment to office, the Grand Master shall serve "ad vitam" until his resignation or removal

Section 5.05.

Upon appointment to office, the High Priest shall serve without fixed term until his resignation or

23

from office. He may resign from office by so notifying both the Dean and the College of Seven in writing.

removal from office. He may resign from office by so notifying both the Chairman of the Council and the Executive Director in writing.

Section 6.06

The Dean of the College may remove the Grand Master from office if he feels that there is just cause for doing so. All voting members of the College, such approval to be communicated to the Grand Master and the Dean, by those College members individually, must approve such a decision in writing.

Section 5.06.

The Chairman of the Council may remove the High Priest from office if he feels that there is just cause for doing so. Such a decision must be approved in writing by at least six other voting members of the Council, such approval to be communicated to the High Priest, the Chairman, and the Executive Director by those Council members individually.

Section 6.07

The Grand Master serves without compensation.

Section 5.07.

The High Priest may serve with or without compensation as determined by the Chairman of the Council. He shall be reimbursed for reasonable expenses involved in carrying out the functions of his office. Determination of reasonable expenses shall be made by the Chairman of the Council.

Article 7. Grand Lodge

Section 7.01

The Grand Lodge is the spiritual nexus of Order Life and Work. The Grand Master and College of Seven are the essential heart of the Grand Lodge, and the members of the College are ipso fact the officers of the Grand Lodge.

Section 7.02

All rights and privileges accorded to the Commanderies and Lodges of the Friary flow from the central authority of the Grand Lodge.

Article 8. Insignia

Section 8.01

Insignia of the Friary shall consist of a gold 8-pointed star, two points upraised. Within the center of the star is a red "Templar Cross." Within the center of the Cross is a sapphire blue orb. All together, this device shall be known as the Signum.

Section 8.02

The insignia described in Section 8.01 may be used by any member of the Friary in accordance with the provisions of this

ARTICLE 9. Insignia

Section 9.01.

Insignia of the Temple of Set shall consist of a pentagram, two points upraised, against a circular field. The edges of the pentagram shall not touch the circular field.

Section 9.02.

The insignia described in Section 9.01 may be used by any member of the Temple of Set in accordance with the

Article, but it shall not be embellished with any other designs or have any other insignia superimposed upon it.

Section 8.03

The various degrees within the Friary are designated by certain ceremonial regalia, as follows:

I) Friars are designated by wearing a white cincture

II) Friars Adeptus Minor are designated by wearing a red cincture

III) Friars Friar Adeptus Major are designated by wearing a yellow cincture and a
white stole.

IV) Magisters Templi are designated by wearing a blue cincture and a blue stole.

V) Members of the College of Seven are designated by wearing the blue cincture of the Fourth degree, and the blue Pallium, instead of the blue stole

VI) The Grand Master is designated by wearing the Grand Master's apron.

provisions of this Article, but it shall not be embellished with any other designs or have any other insignia superimposed upon it.

Section 9.03.

Insignia of the I° shall be a silver pentagram, two points upraised, against a circular field of white.

Section 9.04. Insignia of the II° shall be a silver pentagram, two points upraised, against a circular field of red.

Section 9.05. Insignia of the III° shall be a silver pentagram, two points upraised, against a circular field of black.

Section 9.06. Insignia of the IV° shall be a silver pentagram, two points upraised, against a circular field of blue.

Section 9.07. Insignia of the V° shall be a silver pentagram, two points upraised, against a circular field of purple.

Section 9.08. Insignia of the VI° shall be a silver pentagram, two points upraised, against a circular field of gold.

| Article 9. Commanderies | ARTICLE 10. ORDERS |
|---|---|

**Section 9.01**

The term "Commandery" designates an organizational element of the Friary supervised by one or more IV°+ members as Master/Co-Master of that Commandery. Any IV°+ member may create a Commandery, but may not serve as Master/Co-Master of more than two Commanderies at a time.

**Section 9.02**

The Master/Co-Master of a Commandery exercises complete authority over that Commandery subject to these By-Laws.

**Section 9.03**

Commanderies will accept only II°+ members of the Friary as Commandery members. A member of the Friary may belong to a maximum of one Commandery unless the Masters of that Commandery and any proposed additional Commandery(s) agree that

**Section 10.01.**

The term "Order" designates an organizational element of the Temple of Set supervised by one or more IV°+ members as Grand Master/Co-Grand Masters of that Order. Any IV°+ member may create an Order, but may not serve as Grand Master/Co-Grand Master of more than two Orders at a time.

**Section 10.02.** The Grand Master/Co-Grand Master of an Order exercises complete authority over that Order subject to these By-Laws.

**Section 10.03.**

Orders will accept only II°+ members of the Temple of Set as Order members. A member of the Temple of Set may belong to a maximum of one Order unless the Grand Masters of that Order and any proposed additional Order(s) agree that additional Order membership is acceptable.

additional Commandery membership is acceptable.

Article 10. Lodges

Section 10.01

The term "Lodge" designates an organizational element of the Friary supervised by one or more II°+ members as Sentinel/Co-Sentinels of that Lodge. Any III°+ member may create a Lodge and serve as Sentinel, but may not serve as Sentinel of more than one Lodge at a time. If a II° member is to serve as Sentinel, a III °+ member must sponsor the Lodge.

Section 10.02

The Sentinel/Co-Sentinel of a Lodge exercises complete authority over that Lodge subject to these By-Laws and any policies of the Grand Master concerning Lodges.

Section 10.03

A member of the Friary may belong to a maximum of one Lodge unless the Sentinels of that Lodge and any proposed additional Lodge(s) agree that

ARTICLE 11. Pylons

Section 11.01.

The term "Pylon" designates an organizational element of the Temple of Set supervised by one or more II°+ members as Sentinel/Co-Sentinels of that Pylon. Any III°+ member may create a Pylon and serve as Sentinel, but may not serve as Sentinel of more than one Pylon at a time. If a II° member is to serve as Sentinel, the Pylon must be sponsored by a III°+ member.

Section 11.02. The Sentinel/Co-Sentinel of a Pylon exercises complete authority over that Pylon subject to these By-Laws and any policies of the High Priest concerning Pylons published in the Jeweled Tablets of Set.

Section 11.03.

A member of the Temple of Set may belong to a maximum of one Pylon unless the Sentinels of that Pylon and any proposed additional Pylon(s) agree additional Lodge membership is acceptable.

Article 11. Amendments to By-Laws

Section 11.01

These By-Laws shall become effective immediately upon their adoption. Amendments to these By-Laws shall become effective immediately upon their adoption unless the members in adopting them provide that they are to become effective at a later date.

Section 11.02

These By-Laws may be altered, amended, or repealed and new By-Laws adopted by a simple majority vote of the College of Seven.

Section 11.03

A vote to affect these By-Laws in accordance with Section 11.02 shall be jointly supervised by the Grand Master and the Dean of the College.

that additional Pylon membership is acceptable.

ARTICLE 12. Amendments to By-Laws

Section 12.01.

These By-Laws shall become effective immediately upon their adoption. Amendments to these By-Laws shall become effective immediately upon their adoption unless the members in adopting them provide that they are to become effective at a later date.

Section 12.02.

Subject to any provisions of law applicable to the amendment of By-Laws of non-profit corporations, these By-Laws, or any other of them, may be altered, amended, or repealed and new By-Laws adopted by a three-quarters majority vote of all III°+ members of the Temple of Set.

Section 12.03.

A vote to affect these By-Laws in accordance with Section 12.02 shall be jointly supervised by the High Priest, the Chairman of the Council, and the Executive Director.

29

Section 11.04

The Grand Master may call for a vote to affect these By-Laws in accordance with Section 10.02 at his discretion. A vote must be called for upon receipt by the Dean of a petition signed by no less than three members of the College. Upon receipt of such a petition, the Friary shall immediately cease all programs and activities involving the issue in question until the vote has been conducted, announced, and implemented.

Article 12. Interpretation of By-Laws

Section 12.01

Interpretation of the provisions of these By-Laws, where they are not clearly explicit, shall be by the Grand Master. The Dean of the College may overrule such an interpretation. An overrule decision must be approved in writing by at least four other voting members of the College, such approval to be communicated to the Grand Master and the

Section 12.04.

The High Priest may call for a vote to affect these By-Laws in accordance with Section 12.02 at his discretion. A vote must be called for upon receipt by the Executive Director of a petition signed by one-third of the Active Status III°+ members of the Temple of Set. Upon receipt of such a petition, the Temple of Set shall immediately cease all programs and activities involving the issue in question until the vote has been conducted, announced, and implemented.

ARTICLE 13. Interpretation of By-Laws

Section 13.01.

Interpretation of the provisions of these By-Laws, where they are not clearly explicit, shall be by the High Priest. The Chairman of the Council may overrule such an interpretation. An overrule decision must be approved in writing by at least four other voting members of the Council, such approval to be communicated to the High Priest, the Chairman, and the Executive Director

Dean by those College members individually.

Section 12.02

As used in these By-Laws, the notation "+" following an initiatory degree means "this or any higher degree."

Section 12.03

All degrees of membership and all offices within the Friary may be held by persons of either sex. Use of masculine pronouns in these By-Laws is for simplicity only.

Section 12.04

Any "written notice" referred to in these bylaws may be given in person, sent by postal mail, by commercial courier, facsimile, email, or other commonly used methods of written/typed communication. It is always the responsibility of the sender to ensure that the recipients received the written notice, especially when using methods like email, which are not highly reliable.

Section 12.05

by those Council members individually.

Section 13.02.

As used in these By-Laws, the notation "+" following an initiatory degree means "this or any higher degree."

Section 13.03.

All degrees of membership and all offices within the Priesthood and Temple of Set may be held by persons of either sex. Use of masculine pronouns in these By-Laws is for simplicity only.

[Enacted Grand Master Policy]

In the event of situations arising during a period of time whereby the Office of Dean is vacant, and the College is incomplete, whereby the Friary and its Grandmaster are withheld from acting, operating effectively or efficiently or where bylaws may be viewed as openly contradicting each other during these situations and otherwise (ex: Sections 3.10-11, 4.05,

4.06, 11.04,), the Grand Master shall maintain and remain the sole determinant and enactor of powers held by the College and Dean that cannot be effectively enacted by said Offices and Bodies. This is in concordance with Section 6.01 and 12.01

The similarity between the above sets of By-Laws have a greater impact upon the Friary than one may initially surmise. It may seem of little consequence at first glance, seeing as that they impart no doctrine, theology, or philosophy. However, do not forget that this is a magical order. Foundational documents such as this form the skeletal structure of the body in which the egregore will live and operate. It is therefore not matter of mere legal language being copied over for the sake of convenience. No. When building a structure such as this, utilizing so particular a language cannot but imprint the quality of its source upon the new body. This fact on its own would be enough to claim a definitive Setian influence upon the Friary and AJC. But this is only the psychic construct of organization. The true animating principle, the core philosophy, the raison d'être of the pinnacle of initiation within this body is what we shall reveal and discuss in the next section. It is this animating philosophy that marks the AJC and Friary as definitively left-hand path, and specifically Setian. Let us see why.

# Core Philosophies:
# The Satanic Heart of the AJC

The initiatic summit of the Friary is the Magister/Magistra Templi IV°, as indicated in the above By-Laws. It is therefore to the teachings of this degree that we must turn for an exposition of the doctrine that informs the whole of the order, and by extension, the church. Simply demonstrating the strictly Setian nature of the IV° doctrine will be exceedingly easy. But in order to understand the depth of the deception here, it will be necessary likewise to review and consider some of the concepts it contains, and to show why some of these notions – without making any judgment regarding the correctness of the ideas – are antithetical not only to Christian Gnosticism, but in fact to the Western Mystery Tradition as it has come down to us from antiquity. And most importantly, it represents a philosophical basis which is not only other than what is claimed by the AJC, but is *wholly other*.

Let us look, then, at what is presented to the newly recognized Magister Templi:

# The Masters of the Temple:
# Those who Seek shall Find

You have been Recognized as a Master of the Temple IV°. In terms of organizational authority, you were then and are now familiar with the prerogatives of that degree. They are written into the By-laws, and you have Seen that the Friary will respect them in deed as in word.

To date, however, I have not discussed the essential characteristics of the IV° – the criteria according to which I considered and then recognized you. True, I have discussed various aspects of this with you individually on occasion, but until now, I have not defined the term as comprehensively as it deserves. This I will do now. I do not anticipate that what I say will come as any surprise to you; rather I intend this essay as a way of taking the implicit and making it explicit.

You will notice also that this is the first of my letters addressed only to the IV°. This is because, by definition, only a Master of the Temple may comprehend that grade. Nor may it be "taught" to those of lesser initiatory degrees. Like the II° and the III°, it is something that the individual must seek for himself and attain through the illumination of his Will. Hence the title of this letter: "Those who seek shall find." Thus, again the meaningful use of the term "recognition" as opposed to conferral.

The term "Master" is one of preeminent honor in all of the artistic, religious, and philosophical pursuits of mankind. A Master is one who comprehends, who knows, who possesses all skills. Appropriately, others regard a Master as a teacher, even though he may regard himself as a "student" of his calling. In magick and metaphysics, the Master is one who understands those things which others call "occult" or "mysteries." He may be called a Saint, a Sage, a Mahatma, a Medicine Man, a Shaman, a Witch Doctor, or a Philosopher. Transculturally he is a Master.

Within the initiatory arts of magick to date, Aleister Crowley has most precisely formulated the concept of the Master. Let me cite the key descriptive passages concerning a Master of the Temple (8) = [3] of the A∴A∴ from Magick in Theory and Practice:

"The essential Attainment is the perfect annihilation of that personality which limits and oppresses his true self. The Magister Templi is pre-eminently the Master of Mysticism, that is, His

Understanding is entirely free from internal contradiction or external obscurity; His work is to comprehend the existing Universe in accordance with His own Mind."

When discussing the grade below (8)=[3], that of Adeptus Exemptus (7)=[4], Crowley states:

"He will have attained all but the supreme summits of meditation, and should be already prepared to perceive that the only possible course for him is to devote himself utterly to helping his fellow creatures. To attain the Grade of Magister Templi, he must perform two tasks; the emancipation from thought by putting each idea against its opposite and refusing to prefer either; and the consecration of himself as a pure vehicle for the influence of the order to which he aspires. He must then decide upon the critical adventure of our Order; the absolute abandonment of himself and his attainments."

If you read these passages carefully, you will see the paradox inherent in them. To become an (8) = [3], a (7) = [4] must destroy his capacity for logical thought, i.e. his ability to draw inductive or deductive conclusions from phenomena of the material universe. Since it is just this capacity that is the essential characteristic of the Self ["Cogito ergo sum," if you will], the (7) = [4] is in effect invited to obliterate what it is that makes him a unique entity.

Theoretically he is "reconstituted by the gods in a perfect form" - an ideal "self." Herein lays the heart of the paradox. It is that an independent Will, capable of perceiving itself in contrast to the material Universe, cannot be a product of forces germane to that Universe.

The freedom of the Will necessitates the ability of the Will to move both with and against Universal patterns [i.e. "laws"]. The Will is self-creating, self-sustaining, and self-improving.

Because of the paradox, it is impossible for a Magister Templi (8) = [3] to be the result of such annihilation as Crowley prescribes. Such a "Magister" would possess no Will of its own; it would in fact be a zombie, nonconsciously moving in harmony with the Universal Law. It would be an animated corpse, a mere machine. This would not be rebirth of the self – it would be suicide.

Look at it this way: The Magister Templi is one who can perceive and comprehend the entire material Universe. In order to do this, there must be no part of him that is an accessory of that same Universe. He - his Will - must be independent / separate / distinct. The Magister Templi, if he is truly entitled to that degree, possesses the abilities necessary to thwart those dangers. Those who presume to that degree without understanding them or the severe mental pressures they can cause, do in fact suffer the fate that Crowley prescribes: they either die or lose their sanity.

Crowley had many disciples who can be cited as cases in point. He himself possessed the strength to embody the degree, as well as to exercise the tremendous powers and prerogatives of that exalted station. If Crowley understood the true requirements of a Magister Templi so well, then why should he have misled others via these passages in Magick in Theory and Practice? Intellectually Crowley was brilliant, but invariably his common sense and his sense of perspective would fail him in almost every "category" of his magickal system. He would see trees with unprecedented clarity; he would be blind to forests.

In order to approach the degree of Magister Templi, as it is now constituted within the Friary, let me describe the "forest." First of all, onlookers will note that the first five grades of the Golden Dawn system have given way to the single I°, and the three Adeptus grades [Minor / Major / Exemptus] have given way to the two II° and III°.

A glance through the criteria of the first eight grades of the A∴A∴ will make it quite evident why they were consolidated into the I°, II°, and III°. The nonsense and the blind alleys have been eliminated. The I° now encompasses straightforward training and testing, and the II° is a magical "proving ground" wherein the Adept may exercise his newly acquired strengths and skills. The Adeptus Minor who succeeds in all areas appropriate to his personality may thus be identified as Elect to the III°.

Individuals who are non-Initiates exist both mentally and physically in the material Universe [or objective Universe]. To achieve desired goals they comprehend and employ techniques and devices of the OU only. The I° is shown that there is a perceptual Universe distinct from but relevant to the OU. He is shown that his non-natural mind has the power to alter certain characteristics of the PU, and that such alterations have a somewhat related [but not 1-for-1] impact upon the OU. This is magick. The Adeptus Minor II° is one who is expert at manipulating the PU for desired results in the OU.

However, neither the I° nor the II° really understands what the PU is, or why it exerts the influence that it does on the OU. It is this understanding that constitutes access to the Divine Gift, and it is something that begins with the III°.

The Adeptus Major III° is still a usual "resident" of the OU. He now understands, however, that the PU can embody a reality of its own when energized by the force of his Will [or that of the Will of the Divine]. He can thus "materialize" the PU by his Will, but to do so requires intense concentration and effort on his part – and cannot be sustained for long. The Adeptus Major must still rely upon the automatic laws of the OU to order his thoughts, speech, and actions.

His behavior within the PU is often restricted by his psychological dependence upon the seeming security of the OU. Conversely, his ability to orient himself to the PU may result in his failure to maintain the intricate connections between the OU & PU. In such a case, the PU becomes a mere fantasy world ungoverned by logic and uninfluential with regard to the OU.

Now we are in a position to identify the Magister Templi. The Magister is able to understand the OU completely. He knows what makes it tick, what the forces are that act within it, and how these forces may be manipulated most precisely from the vantage point of the PU. Now we return to that important point raised earlier: A complete understanding of the OU is possible only if the Magister Templi exists as a self-contained entity within the PU. He is necessarily a "detached observer." With this objectivity and this complete freedom from imprisonment within the confines of the OU, the Magister Templi is able to exert his Will upon the OU. He can direct its affairs as they interest him, simply by impressing his Will upon the key determinants in each case. This is not to say that he can make the entire OU "dance to his tune," because his Will is still limited in the amount of data it can consider at any one time and in the focus that it can bring to bear as a result.

Note, however, that the Will of the Magister, while based within the PU for the sake of freedom of action, is still exercised upon the OU. Recall that the Magister is a Master of magick, and that magick is the control of the interrelationship between the PU and the OU.

The Magister Templi no longer "needs" the OU as a psychological prop for his own existence, but it is still the arena in which he acts. It is his ability to conceptualize both the OU and the PU relative to one another that gives him his tremendous power to mold the course of specific events. This is the magician at full strength; this is the force of the individual Will raised to an infinite exponential. This is the Master of the Temple. It is because such qualities are evident in you that you have been recognized as deserving of the IV°.

---

Such is the lesson for the Master of the Temple. Before commenting on certain points of this teaching, we will present, in part, the teaching given to the Magister Templi of the Temple of Set, a teaching which, as you will see presently, is nearly identical to the slightly edited and truncated version given above. Here, then, is the original form of the material, drawn directly from a letter from ToS High Priest Michael Aquino to newly recognized Magisters Templi, as found in the Sapphire Tablet of Set:

## To: The Masters of the Temple

### Qui Petiverent Invenient

On the fifteenth of July X I recognized you as a Master of the Temple IV°. In terms of organizational authority, you were then and are now familiar with the prerogatives of that degree. They are written into the By-laws, and you have Seen that the T S will respect them in deed as in word.

To date, however, I have not discussed the essential characteristics of the IV° – the criteria according to which I considered and then recognized you. True, I have discussed various aspects of this with you individually on occasion, but until now I have not defined the term as comprehensively as it deserves. This I will do now. I do not anticipate that what I will say will come as any surprise to you; rather I intend this letter as a way of taking the implicit and making it explicit.

You will notice also that this is the first of my letters addressed only to the IV°. This is because, by definition, only a Master of the Temple may comprehend that grade. Nor may it be "taught" to those of lesser initiatory degrees. Like the II° and the III°, it is something that the individual must seek for himself and attain through the illumination of his Will. Hence the title of this letter: "Those who seek shall find." And thus again the meaningful use of the term "recognition" as opposed to promotion.

The term "Master" is one of preeminent honor in all of the artistic, religious, and philosophical pursuits of mankind. A Master is one who comprehends, who knows, who possesses all skills. Appropriately a Master is regarded by others as a teacher, even though be may regard himself as a "student" of his calling. In magic and metaphysics, the Master is one who understands those things which others call "occult" or "mysteries". He may be called a Saint, a Sage, a Mahatma, a Medicine Man, a Shaman, a Witch Doctor, or a Philosopher. Transculturally he is a Master.

Within the initiatory arts of magic, the concept of the Master has been most precisely formulated to date by Aleister Crowley. Let me cite the key descriptive passages concerning a Master of the Temple (8)=[3] of the A∴A∴ from Magick in Theory and Practice:

> "The essential Attainment is the perfect annihilation of that personality which limits and oppresses his true self. The Magister

Templi is preeminently the Master of Mysticism, that is, His Understanding is entirely free from internal contradiction or external obscurity; His work is to comprehend the existing Universe in accordance with His own Mind."

When discussing the grade below (8)=[3], that of Adeptus Exemptus (7)=[4], Crowley states:

"He will have attained all but the supreme summits of meditation, and should be already prepared to perceive that the only possible course for him is to devote himself utterly to helping his fellow creatures. To attain the Grade of Magister Templi, he must perform two tasks; the emancipation from thought by putting each idea against its opposite, and refusing to prefer either; and the consecration of himself as a pure vehicle for the influence of the order to which he aspires. He must then decide upon the critical adventure of our Order; the absolute abandonment of himself and his attainments."

And further:

"Should he fail, by will or weakness, to make his self-annihilation absolute, he is none the less thrust forward into the Abyss; but instead of being received and reconstructed in the Third Order, as a Babe in the womb of our Lady Babalon, under the night of Pan, to grow up to be Himself wholly and truly as He was not previously, he remains in the Abyss, secreting his elements round his Ego as if isolated from the Universe, and becomes what is called a "Black Brother". Such a being is gradually disintegrated from lack of nourishment and the slow but certain action of the attraction of the rest of the Universe, despite his now desperate efforts to insulate and protect himself, and to aggrandize himself by predatory practices. He may indeed prosper for awhile, but in the end he must perish, especially when with a new Aeon a new Word is proclaimed which he cannot and will not hear, so that he is handicapped by trying to use an obsolete method of Magick, like a man with a boomerang in a battle where everyone else has a rifle."

If you read these passages carefully, you will see the paradox inherent in them. To become an (8)=[3], a (7)=[4] must destroy his capacity for logical thought, i.e. his ability to draw inductive or deductive conclusions from phenomena of the material universe. Since it is just this capacity that is the essential characteristic of the Self ["Cogito ergo sum", if you will], the (7)=[4] is in effect invited to obliterate what it is that makes him a unique entity. Theoretically he is "reconstituted by the gods in a perfect form" - an ideal "self". Herein lies the heart of the paradox, which is also the central theme of Genesis III. It is that an independent Will, capable of perceiving itself in contrast to the material Universe, cannot be a product of forces germane to that Universe. The freedom of the Will necessitates the ability of the Will to move both with and against Universal patterns [i.e. "laws"]. The Will is self-creating, self-sustaining, and self-improving. This is the basis for the Formula of the Aeon of Set XXX.

Because of the paradox, it is impossible for a Magister Templi (8)=[3] to be the result of such an annihilation as Crowley prescribes. Such a "Magister" would possess no Will of its own; it would in fact be a zombie, nonconsciously moving in harmony with the Universal Law. It would be an animated corpse, a mere machine. This would not be rebirth of the self – it would be suicide.

Now let us look a little more closely at Crowley's description of a "Black Brother". If you have read Crowley's biography, you will notice something very significant: that, in these few short phrases, a veritable blueprint for Crowley's own life has been presented. [This is not the case in Moonchild, incidentally, where the term "Black Brother" is used to lampoon Crowley's old Golden Dawn opponents.]

Anyone familiar with Crowley's writings as a Magister Templi (8)=[3] onward can attest to the tremendous presence of his individual Will. The inescapable conclusion is that there is no Right-Hand Path to the degree of Magister Templi. There is only the Left- Hand Path, and it is fraught with danger – not a one-time test, but a continuous peril that exists from the moment the individual completely realizes him-self as a Magister.

Look at it this way: The Magister Templi is one who can perceive and comprehend the entire material Universe. In order to do this, there must be no part of him which is an accessory of that same Universe. He - his Will - must be independent / separate / distinct. This necessitates an extremely strong presence of mind, an ego that is sufficiently reinforced by itself not to require "crutches" from the material Universe, and a determination to fight off the panic that could result from the sensation of being utterly alone. The Magister Templi, if he is truly entitled to that degree, possesses the abilities necessary to thwart those dangers. Those who presume to that degree without understanding them or the severe mental pressures they can cause, do in fact suffer the fate that Crowley prescribes: they either die or lose their sanity.

Crowley had many disciples who can be cited as cases in point. He himself possessed the strength to embody the degree, as well as to exercise the tremendous powers and prerogatives of that exalted station. The difficulties that he suffered in later life were the result of other factors [specifically the Curse of the degree of Magus, and Crowley's decision to assume the dangerous perspective of an Ipsissimus ... these I will discuss later.] If Crowley understood the true requirements of a Magister Templi so well, then why should he have misled others via these passages in Magick in Theory and Practice? The answer, I think, lies not in Crowley himself, but rather in the general atmosphere of inconsistency and imperfection that permeated the Aeon of HarWer. Intellectually Crowley was brilliant, but invariably his common sense and his sense of perspective would fail him in almost every "category" of his magical system. He would see trees with unprecedented clarity; he would be blind to forests. Such was the unfortunate atmosphere of the Aeon of HarWer.

In order to approach the degree of Magister Templi as it is now constituted within the Aeon of Set, let me describe the "forest". First of all, onlookers will note that the first five grades of the Golden Dawn system have given way to the single I° T S , and the three Adeptus grades [Minor / Major / Exemptus] have given way to the single II° T S . Also the Priesthood of Set III° has been added – a credential entirely alien to the nonunified atmosphere of the Aeon of HarWer.

A glance through the criteria of the first eight grades of the A∴A∴ will make it quite evident why they were consolidated into the I° and II°. The nonsense and the Cabalistic blind alleys have been eliminated. The I° now encompasses straight-forward training and testing, and the II° is a magical "proving ground" wherein the Adept may exercise his newly-acquired strengths and skills. The Adept who succeeds in all areas appropriate to his personality may thus be identified as Elect to the Priesthood.

Individuals who are non-Setians exist both mentally and physically in the material Universe [or objective Universe]. To achieve desired goals they comprehend and employ techniques and devices of the OU only. The Setian I° is shown that there is a perceptual Universe distinct from but relevant to the OU. He is shown that his nonnatural mind has the power to alter certain characteristics of the PU, and that such alterations have a somewhat related [but not 1-for-1] impact upon the OU. This is magic. The Adept II° is one who is expert at manipulating the PU for desired results in the OU. But neither the I° nor the II° really understands what the PU is, or why it exerts the influence that it does on the OU. It is this understanding that constitutes access to the Powers of Darkness, and it is something that begins with the III°.

The Priest III° is still a usual "resident" of the OU. He now understands, however, that the PU can embody a reality of its own when energized by the force of his Will [or that of the Will of Set]. He can thus "materialize" the PU by his Will, but to do so requires intense concentration and effort on his part – and cannot be sustained for long. The Priest must still rely upon the automatic laws of the OU to order his thoughts, speech, and actions. His behavior within the PU is often restricted by his psychological dependence upon the seeming security of the OU. Or, conversely, his ability to orient himself to the PU may result in his failure to maintain the intricate connections between the OU & PU. In such a case, the PU becomes a mere fantasy world ungoverned by logic and uninfluential with regard to the OU. [This is the well-known "Astral Plane" phenomenon.]

Now we are in a position to identify the Magister Templi. The Magister is able to understand the OU completely. He knows what makes it tick, what the forces are that act within it, and how these forces may be manipulated most precisely from the vantage point of the PU. Now we return to that important point raised earlier: A complete understanding of the OU is possible only if the Magister Templi exists as a self-contained entity within the PU. He is necessarily a "detached observer". With this objectivity and this complete freedom from imprisonment within the confines of the OU, the Magister Templi is able to exert his Will upon the OU with absolute impunity. He can direct its affairs as they interest him, simply by impressing his Will upon the key determinants in each case. This is not to say that he can make the entire OU "dance to his tune," because his Will is still limited in the amount of data it can consider at any one time and in the focus that it can bring to bear as a result. But the Magister can direct his attention wherever he wishes in the OU, and the results of his efforts will be uniformly successful in each case.

Note, however, that the Will of the Magister, while based within the PU for the sake of freedom of action, is still exercised upon the OU. Recall that the Magister is a Master of magic, and that magic is the control of the interrelationship between the PU and the OU. The Magister Templi no longer "needs" the OU as a psychological prop for his own existence, but it is still the arena in which he acts. It is his ability to conceptualize both the OU and the PU relative to one another that gives him his tremendous power to mold the course of specific events. This is the magician at full strength; this is the force of the individual Will raised to an infinite exponential. This is the Master of the Temple of Set. It is because such qualities are evident in you that you have been recognized as deserving of the IV°.

---

So, there you have it. The innermost doctrine of the Friary/OSF/AJC is a letter from Michael Aquino to those who have recently attained the IV° Magister Templi in the Temple of Set – minus a few references to the ToS itself, as well as to the left-hand path. But removing the words "Temple of Set" or "left-hand path" does not alter the doctrine in the least.

Now, to be clear, our issue is not at all with the Temple of Set; nor is it even with the doctrines they espouse. Certainly, I could discuss the merits and shortcomings I perceive within the Setian doctrine. But this is not the medium for such an exercise. And even were we to undertake that endeavor, it would be conducted fraternally and respectfully. And I expect that the Temple of Set would put forth their best arguments and defend them vigorously, honestly.

No, the issue here goes back to what we discussed near the beginning of our investigation. Remember the AJC's response to accusations of Satanism? They claimed that its founding was far removed from any such philosophy or activity, that the founders had nothing to do with any such works, "nor did any of the beliefs, values or rituals of the associated path or organization form the basis of the Apostolic Johannite Church." Hmm... are you sure about that? Well, they must be, because they double down:

> **The Apostolic Johannite Church has never been, is not now, nor will ever be Satanic, nor for that matter is it associated with any organizations of a left-hand path or Satanic character.**

Do you begin to see now the blatant lie here? This is the face of evil. The Setian doctrine? Oh, I believe it to be flawed. But the evil is not in the espousal of the doctrine. The evil is in the outright denial of the manifest facts; the brazen deception committed against all those who would come seeking the Christian Gnosis but are unwittingly feeding an egregore that seems diametrically opposed to the most fundamental aspects of Christianity.

So, is it possible to propagate a left-hand path Christianity? Perhaps. And if that is what the AJC wants to do, then they should just be honest about it. But deception is in the very fabric of the church. It has been there from the beginning as a dark, seething leviathan insinuating its tendrils of corruption into the hearts of its most senior leadership.

Now, I know that I said I wouldn't debate the merits of Setian doctrine here. But this study would not be complete without at least addressing some principal points and showing how the Setian doctrine is indeed at odds, in some respects, with nearly every form of Christian mysticism, including Gnosticism.

The foremost point of disagreement between the Setian philosophy and that of Gnosticism, Christian mysticism, and the Western Mysteries in general, lies in the concept of deification. Both schools of thought seek a form of deification, to be sure. But while the Christian mystic who follows the Way of the Heart of Saint-Martin, or the Operative Way of Pasqually and Willermoz, or, like many of us, some combination of the two, seeks Reintegration, the Setian or left-hand path seeks the exact opposite – a supreme separation. The Christian mystic seeks Theosis. The Satanic mystic seeks Apotheosis.

My intention was, at this point, to cite a previous work of mine which addresses this very issue. But rather than pulling excerpts from the work, it seems better to include the entire piece as an appendix. This discussion of deification is of the utmost relevance to the topic at hand, and of the greatest importance to the Christian occultist. The varying opinions are not merely a matter of hair-splitting. There are deep theological implications attached to the various viewpoints. So, we will leave this discussion alone for the moment, referring you to the appendix for a deeper study. It will be noted only that the reference in the essay to a "fairly well known so-called Christian Gnostic church" may now be identified as none other than the Apostolic Johannite Church.

# Final Thoughts

In closing, I will state merely that the preparation of this monograph has not brought me joy, as do my other publishing projects. It is necessary, certainly, and has been for many years. And for many years I have kept my head down, focusing on my own myriad shortcomings, studying, praying, writing, and translating. But the venomous hostility hurled relentlessly and mercilessly against not only me, but against any who dare call me "Brother" has moved me to finally declare that the emperor has no clothes.

The depth of the deceit, fraud, and hypocrisy perpetrated by these charlatans would make a carnival hawker blush. And those who had a front row seat along with me to the statements and actions of some of these "righteous" men know that

I haven't even scratched the surface here. But it is not necessary that I set forth all the evidence I've accumulated. My intent is not to disgust the reader or make them recoil in horror (which some of the information I have surely would). No, the little I've presented here is more than enough to illustrate the larger points.

To the sincere seeker among the AJC: be aware. Be aware of what you're feeding your energy into. Become knowledgeable about your origins and the inner teachings which form the spiritual engine of the church. Above all, let love be your guide. Whether you embrace these revelations or reject them, do so in the spirit of love and reconciliation. Do not become fodder for a hate-fueled machine.

# Theosis Through Gnosis

## Gnostic Considerations on Deification

*(reprinted from the Apostolic Church of the Pleroma Clergy Handbook)*

Theosis is a term employed largely by the Eastern Orthodox church to describe the divinization of Man (i.e. humanity). This doctrine of divinization or deification is derived from the Second Epistle of Peter, chapter 1, verse 4, which exhorts us to "become partakers of the divine nature." Within Eastern Orthodoxy this doctrine is of such vital and central importance that it is often equated with salvation and the very purpose of Life itself. We, as Gnostic Christians, of course have no quarrel with this worthy pursuit. In fact, in this regard the ultimate aims of the Gnostic and Orthodox Christian are fundamentally identical. This is not to say that our theological doctrines are identical, but our approaches to theology are similar in that they derive from mystical revelation rather than the pure rational speculation of Catholic Scholasticism. Let us, therefore, look at this process known as theosis through the lens of Gnosticism, as well as its scriptural sources and means of attainment.

According to the doctrine of theosis, deification is attained through a three stage process: Catharsis (καθαρσις) or Purification; Theoria (θεωρια) or Illumination; and Theosis (θεωσις), which term thus describes the process as a whole, as well as the final stage of that process. This final stage represents the regeneration of humanity to its primitive estate, which is divine. This, however, poses some challenges to

61

Orthodox theology, for they hold that God is transcendent and that His essence is unknowable. But the genuine mystical experience proves to the participant empirically that there is a divinity immanent in Man. In order to reconcile these seemingly contradictory views, theologians such as Gregory Palamas have posited that there is a distinction between the "essence" of God - which remains unknowable, and the "energies" or "operations" of God, through which it is possible to obtain an experiential knowledge of God. This is not an altogether bad explanation, as it is easily relatable to the principles of the *fixed* and the *volatile* as in the alchemical Sulphur & Mercury. In the Orthodox schema, the "essence" would be the Sulphuric or *fixed* aspect of God; that is, it remains within Himself, unchangeable and immovable. The "energies" would be the Mercurial or *volatile* aspect, with which we may participate and ultimately unite our consciousness. Many western theologians, however - especially those who adhere to the school of Scholasticism - have viewed this as an irreconcilable division within God.

The Gnostic, on the other hand, asserts the fundamental unity of God. One may still use the words "essence" and "energies" as semantic conventions if it seems helpful, but the doctrines of Gnosticism show that there is a solution that is both simple and elegant. Most branches of modern Gnosticism, while having very little dogma to speak of, mostly agree on two fundamental doctrines: the doctrine of emanation; and salvation through gnosis. We will address the second doctrine a little further on. But let us now look briefly at the doctrine of emanation.

*Emanation* means a pouring or issuing forth as a means of generation, as opposed to *creation* which is the forming and fashioning of a thing using some outside medium. The concept of creation works fine on the lower planes. For example, humans create by fashioning things of a material nature, utilizing the elements of the material universe. Even seemingly incorporeal things, such as music, consist of generating particular vibratory patterns within the medium of air. If there were no air, liquid, or solid medium through which these vibrations could be generated, then it would be impossible to create sound or music. We may even extend this analogy to the astral or psychic realm wherein the Demiurge and his archons create worlds using substances of which they themselves are not the source. But this theory becomes problematic once we have worked our way back to the source, i.e. God Himself. God, as the ultimate Source of all, cannot have created in the sense of the manipulation of some outside material, since He must necessarily be the very source of any such material. This paradox is resolved in creation doc- trine by the introduction of the concept of *creatio ex nihilo*, creation from nothing.

Emanation on the other hand, posits a process of the issuing forth of the Aeons - the whole of the Pleroma. In Gnostic thought, God - who is sometimes called the One - reflects upon itself, resulting in the emanation of Thought, or First Thought (Protennoia). This is the Holy Spirit of the Trinity. Through this Thought, the One then issues forth the Logos. The Logos, just as the Thought, was pre-existent in the Father (Propator), and is in fact the creative power of the Father. The Logos, therefore, is seen to issue forth of its own accord, and is thus not only Monogenes (alone-born, or only begotten), but also Autogenes (self-generated). It is by means of the Logos, then, that all subsequent realities or hypostases are brought forth. The Trinity, therefore, existed in union with the Father, or the One, for all eternity; and their emanation or issuing forth makes them no less substantively or essentially divine, but it does make that divinity accessible, as we shall attempt to explain.

Adam was made a "living soul" through the infusion of *pneuma*, or spirit - the very essence of the divine. And it is only because of the immanence of the divine essence in Man that we may hope to gain an experiential knowledge (gnosis) of the transcendent Father. If, therefore, we see God as *both* transcendent and immanent, we no longer need to draw any substantive distinction between the "essence" and "energies" of God, except as semantic conveniences to help better explain our relative and conditional experience of God in contrast to the fullness of God in His boundlessness.

Before we get ahead of ourselves, let us return to an examination of the three stages of Theosis: Catharsis, Theoria, and Theosis proper. Catharsis, as previously stated, is a stage of purification. Orthodox theology holds that this purification is most importantly the purification of consciousness. This purification is effected through various means of asceticism. Among the advanced initiates of the Mystery Traditions, this purification through asceticism constitutes a phase of spiritual alchemy.

Among the Orthodox, this purification is brought about chiefly through the practice of Hesychasm. In both instances the practitioner seeks to cultivate "ceaseless prayer" (cf. *1 Thess.* 5:17), which is also known as "Prayer of the Heart." This contemplative prayer arises from a state of perpetual watchfulness, or nepsis (Gr. νεψις).

The basis of Hesychasm, from-the Greek *hesuchos* (ἡσυχος, quiet, silent), is found in *Matthew* 6:6, "Whenever you pray, go into your hidden room and shut the door and pray to your Father who is in secret." This is understood to mean that one is to retire unto oneself, the heart being that "hidden room." This doctrine is not at odds with the Gnostic *Gospel of Philip* which states, "He said, 'Go into your room, shut the door behind you, and pray to your Father who is in secret,' that is, the one who is innermost. What is innermost is the Fullness, and there is nothing further within. And this is what they call the uppermost."

Hesychasm involves asceticism and repetitive prayer, usually the so-called Jesus Prayer: "Lord Jesus Christ, Son of God, have mercy on me, a sinner." Through the repeated recitation of the Jesus Prayer, one may be brought to the awareness and experience of the true inner prayer, or Prayer of the Heart. Another prayer utilized since antiquity is the one given by St. John Cassian (c. 360-435): "O God, make speed to save me. O Lord, make haste to help me." Hesychasm also involves adopting certain postures and breathing techniques. Students of the ACP formation program - all initiates in fact - should appreciate the use of breathing, posture, and intonation as a means toward inner illumination. These practices, of course, do not actually cause the state of inner illumination. They are merely part of the preparatory and purgative process that allows for the eventual liberation of conscience from the fetters of the temporal passions. The actual inner illumination is known as theoria, which we shall now discuss.

Theoria is the word from which our word "theory" is derived. It is from the verb *theorein*, meaning "to look at, consider, speculate, contemplate." Its meaning in Orthodox theology, however, as well as within Neoplatonism, is closer to the Latin *contemplatio* than *speculatio*. That is, it is understood to refer to the inner, contemplative, primary experiential knowledge that leads to divine union, rather than the speculative, secondary or tertiary knowledge that arises through rational inquiry. The theological conception of theoria moves even beyond its use by the Neoplatonists, from whom it was borrowed. According to Thomas Keating, the Church Fathers viewed theoria as being akin to the Hebrew word *da'ath* implying an experiential knowledge not of the mind alone, but of the mind united with the heart, involving the whole being. In short, theoria should be understood to have the sense of "beholding" rather than merely "thinking of."

One of the chief proponents and defenders of Hesychasm and the doctrine of theosis in general was St. Gregory Palamas (1296-1359), who taught that theoria is the state of beholding the uncreated Light of God, the "Tabor Light." This doctrine states that the light that shone at the transfiguration of Jesus on Mount Tabor (Mt. 17, Mk. 9, Lk. 9:28-), identified also with the light seen by St. Paul at his conversion, is that very uncreated Light of God which is not the essence of God, but emanates perpetually from that essence, and is inseparable from the divine essence itself. Palamas went to great lengths to emphasize the distinction between the essence of God, which is eternal and uncreated and transcendent, and the energies of God, which are also eternal and uncreated and, as we have seen, inseparable from the essence, but accessible. Furthermore, Palamas theorized that the Tabor Light is one and the same as the promised Kingdom of Heaven. In fact, this is one of the theses of Palamas that was canonized by the Orthodox church.

*Luke* 17:20b-21 states: "The Kingdom of God is not coming with that which can be observed; nor will they say 'Behold, here it is!' or 'There it is!' For behold, the Kingdom of God is within you!" If, therefore, the Tabor Light is one and the same as the Kingdom (as affirmed by Orthodox canon), and if the Kingdom is within, that is, immanent (as affirmed by the very words of Jesus), then it follows that that uncreated Light which shone forth from Jesus at the Transfiguration is in fact immanent within every human.

Orthodoxy, while allowing for the possibility of a "true gnosis," most often likes to distance itself from the term "gnosis" or at least to accord it a rank lower than theoria. The following passage from the "Palamism" entry in Wikipedia describes this pretty well:

Gnosis and all knowledge are created, as they are derived or created from experience, self-awareness and spiritual knowledge. Theoria, here, is the experience of the uncreated in various degrees, i.e. the vision of God or to see God. The experience of God in the eighth day or outside of time therefore transcends the self and the experiential knowledge or gnosis. Gnosis is most importantly understood as a knowledge of oneself; theoria is the experience of God, transcending the knowledge of oneself.

This idea is summed up succinctly in the Wiki for "Theoria" which states: "Knowledge is derived from experience, but experience is not derived from knowledge." In other words, theoria, or experience of God, is seen as the primary or causative event, and gnosis - however genuine and pure it may be - can only be a secondary event; an effect of the experience. This is a very clever argument, and one that initially appears quite convincing. But this definition of gnosis is rather limiting, not only according to a Gnostic interpretation, but even within orthodox circles, such as the statements by Thomas Keating previously mentioned which readily equate theoria with da'ath (knowledge). The problem is that the term gnosis is used by the theologians to mean different things at different times. In one instance it may mean the intellectual knowledge gained through rational inquiry; in another case it may refer to the knowledge of oneself; and yet again it may be used to refer to spiritual knowledge, but which is separate from and subsequent to the spiritual experience itself. But Gnosis, to the Gnostic, is a revelatory knowledge which is indistinguishable from the experience itself. Gnosis, therefore, to the Gnostic, is in fact the same phenomenon as that called theoria by the Orthodox.

Of the three types of knowledge referred to above, the first is dealing with a mundane form of knowledge. The third form refers only to the memory of an experience. But the second type - knowledge of oneself - comes closer to what we, as Gnostics, mean by the term gnosis. Gnostics often distinguish, however, between personal gnosis and divine gnosis. It is generally held that personal gnosis is but a step toward the divine gnosis. We have already shown that theoria, or divine gnosis, is the vision or realization of the immanence of the divine. So, if God is immanent, or "innermost" as stated in the *Gospel of Philip*, then the knowledge of oneself, through maturation and cultivation, may lead to the experience of God - divine gnosis/theoria, which in turn leads ultimately to theosis, or union with God.

While we feel that we have successfully argued in favor of equating gnosis with theoria, it will be better to offer additional scriptural support for our assertions. Let us turn, then, to *2 Peter* - the very scripture on which the entire doctrine of theosis is based. This epistle is a particularly mystical text in which references to gnosis are found throughout. In fact, gnosis is one of the very first things mentioned, and one of the very last things mentioned. And sandwiched in between among these three short chapters are a number of mystical treasures.

As early as the 2nd verse of the first chapter, we read: "May grace and peace be multiplied unto you in knowledge of God and Jesus our Lord." So, right from the start we are reading of the "knowledge of God." The text continues in verse 3:

> All things for life and godliness have been given to us by His divine power through the knowledge of the One Who called us to His own glory and virtue.

We see here, then, that lest there be any mistake concerning the value of the knowledge mentioned in verse 2, it is nothing less than the "divine power" that comes to us "through knowledge." And this divine power enables us to receive life (ζωη - zoe; not mere *bios*) and godliness. We therefore now see the context in which the following verse occurs - the verse, as stated previously, which constitutes the scriptural basis for the doctrine of theosis:

> Through which things he has given us the precious and great promises, that through these you may become participants of the divine nature, having escaped the cosmos which has been corrupted by lust.

It now becomes clear that the "things he has given us" that allow us to "become participants of the divine nature" are the "knowledge of God" and the "divine power" that comes through that knowledge. Therefore, if theosis is participation in the divine nature, and if theoria is the means by which theosis is attained, then we must conclude that theoria consists of the knowledge of God and the divine power that comes through this knowledge. But let us continue with our study of the text.

The next verses show us that knowledge does not

operate in a vacuum. Rather, it is part of a process that culminates in deification, the crowning virtue of which is agape. Thus we read in verses 5-7:

And for this very reason, you must with due diligence support faith with virtue, and virtue with knowledge, and knowledge with self-control, and self-control with endurance, and endurance with godliness, and godliness with brotherly love (φιλαδελφια - philadelphia), and brotherly love with agape (αγαπη).

We must therefore always remember that gnosis, however precious it may be, is not an end unto itself, but a part of the process toward divinization. We do posit, however, that it is the central and key experience of the divinization process. And our scripture seems to bear this out, for we read in the very next verses ( 8-9):

> For these things being in you and multiplying keep you from becoming un- productive and unfruitful in the knowledge of our Lord Jesus Christ. For anyone in whom these things are not present is shortsighted and blind, having forgotten the purification [καθαρισμου] of his past shortcomings [άμαρτιων].

We have thus once again returned to our central theme of knowledge, which comes after a period of purification or catharsis. This gives us even further evidence to identify gnosis as the principal experience of theoria. Now, we will not here provide an exegesis of every verse of this epistle, but let us continue on for a while, for the next two verses (10-11) offer continued support to our thesis:

Therefore, brothers, be diligent to confirm your calling and election, for in doing these things you will not ever fall. For thus will be richly provided for you the entrance into the eternal kingdom [αιωνιον βασιλειαν] of our Lord and Savior Jesus Christ.

There are a number of interesting points contained in these verses. First, in verse 10 we see reference to the "calling and election." We don't wish to go too far into this here, but these terms are significant to Gnostic theology, as they are seen to represent the psychic church and the pneumatic church, sometimes referred to as the Church Suffering and the Church Triumphant. In verse 11, though, we find concepts directly pertinent to our study. Here the text speaks of entry into the eternal kingdom. You will recall that the Kingdom has already been identified with the uncreated Light of God (according to Orthodox canon), and that the Kingdom is immanent (according to *Luke* 17:20-21). If we look at the Greek words which we translate as "eternal kingdom" αιωνιον βασιλειαν – we could also read this as "the Kingdom of the Aeons." In other words, through gnosis we may access the Pleroma. Recall the previously quoted text from the *Gospel of Philip*: "What is innermost is the Fullness [i.e. Pleroma], and there is nothing further within. And this is what they call the uppermost."

As if to reaffirm the correctness of this doctrine, verses 17-18 tell us:

> He [Jesus] received honor and glory from God the Father when that voice was conveyed to him by the Majestic Glory, saying, "This is my Son, my Beloved, with whom I am well pleased." We

ourselves heard this voice come from heaven, while we were with him on the holy mountain.

The text, in recalling here the Tabor event, does indeed seem to confirm the whole doctrine of theosis, in both its Orthodox and Gnostic aspects. But it is within the next verse (19) that we find the summation of this process so beautifully expressed:

> So we have the prophetic message more fully confirmed. You will do well to be attentive to this as a lamp shining in a dark place, until the day dawns and the Morning Star rises in your hearts.

We have written elsewhere concerning this passage and the meaning of the Morning Star. In our treatise, "Morning Star Rising" we have stated that the "rising of the Morning Star...in one's heart is a reference to the emergence of the Light of Gnosis within the individual." Let us expand on this concept a bit further by revisiting a longer excerpt from that work:

> The grace that comes from Christ's sacrifice is accessible through faith. But the Morning Star is obtainable only through gnosis, to those who conquer their lower natures by a concerted act of Will, and who accomplish the Work of Jesus, as we read in the Revelation of St. John:
>
>> To everyone who conquers and continues to do my works to the end, I will give authority over the nations...even as I also received authority from my Father. To the one who conquers I will also give the Morning Star. Let anyone who has an ear listen to what the Spirit is saying to the churches, (Rev. 2:26, 28-29).

73

We are told near the end of Revelation that the Morning Star is in fact Jesus Christ himself:

It is I, Jesus, who sent my angel to you with this testimony for the churches. I am the root and the descendant of David, the bright and Morning Star, (Rev. 22:16).

This is a most intriguing statement, and one that requires comment on a couple of fronts. First, as we have just said, it definitively identifies the Morning Star with Jesus himself. But we must look at this title as more than a mere epithet of Christ. Given its other canonical usage in *2 Peter*, wherein it is described as something to rise within, and in the second chapter of *Revelation* wherein it is something that is granted from on high to "the one who conquers," we must conclude that this title refers to a state of being, of existence, which may be attained by the initiate who overcomes the trials and Ordeals. Indeed, we must conclude that the Morning Star refers to the very state of Christhood. To put this into a Qabalistic context, it is the consciousness that has ascended to Tiphareth, and furthermore has attained the Knowledge and Conversation of the Holy Guardian Angel. This is not to say that the consciousness has achieved reintegration into the Pleroma, but that reintegration is now possible. In other words, the arising of the Morning Star is that Gnostic illumination sought by every initiate of the Mysteries; true Salvation.

Certainly, more could be said on this verse alone (2 Peter 1:19), but we need to move along with the study of our topic. The second chapter of 2 Peter is de- voted largely to admonishments to stay upon the true path and warning of the dire consequences of straying. But the profundity of this chapter reaches its climax toward the final verses. Before examining these verses, though, let us turn to Luke 12:10, wherein we read of the enigmatic "blaspheme of the Holy Spirit":

> Everyone who speaks a word against the Son of Man will be forgiven, but whoever blasphemes against the Holy Spirit will not be forgiven.

You may wonder why, in the midst of our study of theosis, we would turn to such an obscure and puzzling topic as the blaspheme of the Holy Spirit, or the "unforgivable sin." But it is in fact directly related to our topic, and is explained in *2 Peter* 2:20-21, thus:

> If, after they have escaped the defilements of the cosmos through knowledge of our Lord and Savior Jesus Christ, they are again entangled in them and defeated, for them the last state has become worse than the first. For it was better for them not to have known the way of righteousness than, having known it, to turn away from the holy commandment that was passed on to them.

We see, therefore, the singular importance placed on the attainment and retention of the "knowledge of our Lord." So central is it to the process of salvation (deification) that to obtain it and then reject it puts the soul in a mortal danger worse than its original spiritual ignorance. The Gnostics of old held this precise view, for we read in the *Secret Book of John*:

> I said, "Lord, where will the souls go of people who had knowledge but turned away?"

He said to me, "They will be taken to the place where the angels of misery go, where there is no repentance. They will be kept there until the day when those who have blasphemed against the Spirit will be tortured and punished eternally."

This passage shows us that the ancients viewed this phenomenon as being identical to the blaspheme of the Holy Spirit. The *Pistis Sophia* also addresses this:

All men who shall receive the mysteries of the Ineffable - blessed indeed are the souls which shall receive of those mysteries; but if they turn and transgress and come out of the body before they have repented, the judgment of those men is sorer than all the judgments, and it is exceedingly violent... they will be cast into the outer darkness and perish and be non-existent forever.

Truly, it is difficult to imagine how such a transgression could even occur; to attain to such limitless heights only to be dragged back into a state of willful ignorance. But the emphasis given to this phenomenon in both canonical and Gnostic scriptures assures us that this is a very real condition, and that we must maintain our watchfulness diligently. This is the same watchfulness, or sobriety - nepsis - spoken of previously that leads to the contemplative "Prayer of the Heart."

The third chapter of *2 Peter* deals mainly with the dawning of the awaited illumination. It speaks of the burning away of the temporal, or elemental things of the world, and the coming of the "day of the Lord" and the "new heavens and new earth." These are terms used to refer to the coming of the Kingdom of God which, of course, does not refer to the destruction of the physical cosmos, but to the transformation of consciousness brought about by beholding the Light of Christ. Again, we are not going to give·.an exegesis of this final chapter, but we do want to draw your attention to the final verse of the text:

> Grow in the grace and knowledge of our Lord and Savior Jesus Christ. To him be the glory both now and to the day of eternity. Amen.

We really only want to make a couple of comments on this verse. First, we find the concept of gnosis reiterated once again. The text really could not be more clear on the matter. It opens in the first chapter with a discussion of knowledge as the means by which we receive divine power and partake in the divine nature. The theme of the knowledge of God is then reiterated throughout the whole text. And then we find it emphasized once again in the concluding verse, as if to re-mind us that it is the beginning and ending of all spiritual works. As a secondary comment on this verse, it is interesting to note that the phrase translated as "day of eternity" or "day of the age" is more appropriately rendered: as the "day of the Aeon" (Gr. ἡμεραν αιωνος ).

We have nearly exhausted our study of theoria, but before moving on let us examine another aspect. Up to this point we have mentioned the path of asceticism or the Prayer of the Heart, as a means toward theoria or illumination. But there is also the sacramental path, which is equally important to the attainment of illumination and eventual deification. Referring once again to the "Theoria" Wiki, it states:

> While theoria is possible through prayer, it is attained in a perfect way through the Eucharist. Perfect vision of the deity, perceptible in its uncreated light, is the "mystery of the eighth day." The eighth day is the day of the Eucharist but it also has an eschatological dimension as it is the day outside of the week i.e. beyond time. It is the start of a new eon of human history. Through the Eucharist people experience the eternity of God who transcends time and space.

This is also a doctrine held by many modern Gnostics. Robert Ambelain (Tau Jean III), late Patriarch of the Église Gnostique Apostolique (Gnostic Apostolic Church), states in his work *Spiritual Alchemy*:

> With the Eucharist, we absorb an occult and mystic "charge," a *philter of immortality* which, if we impregnate ourselves with it sufficiently and often enough during the course of our terrestrial life, could transmute us little by little, year by year. For this "charge," assimilated by our organism like all regular nourishment, nevertheless passes from the physiological plane to the psyche, and from the psyche into the *nous*, or spirit.

We see, therefore, that the sacramental life is not supplanted by the ascetic life, but neither does it supplant the ascetic life. But through adherence to both ascetic and sacramental practices, one may hope to obtain the perfect vision of God. And it is this vision, this beholding of the Tabor Light, that leads one into full theosis - the regenerated Man.

So what is meant, precisely, by deification or divinization? A simple answer would be that it is to become one with God. This answer would not be disputed by either the Orthodox or the Gnostic. It does, however, have certain implications that could suggest an incompatibility with Orthodox dogma. For example, Orthodoxy emphasizes that becoming divine through theosis is not the same as the doctrine of apotheosis, or becoming "a God" such as may be found within Mormonism and some forms of Satanism (e.g. Setianism - not to be confused with Sethianism!). Apotheosis is considered as a heresy in the Orthodox church, and I am inclined to agree with that position. The goal of every true mystic is to achieve union with the divine. The erroneous doctrine of apotheosis asserts that the individual may be raised, or may raise oneself, to such a stature that he becomes for all intents and purposes co-eternal and co-omnipotent with God, or the divine essence, yet remaining as an utterly unique hypostasis, divorced from the influences of the supreme creative principle. Hence, in this doctrine any union with the divine is merely a steppingstone by which one may increase his or her power and knowledge in order to ultimately break free of the natural order. This doctrine is precisely (if over-simplified) that of the Temple of Set, an off-shoot of the Church of Satan.

Many Gnostics, if not most (certainly those who have been educated and trained in the mystical orders and societies traditionally associated with the Gnostic Church) will recognize immediately the fallacies contained within the above doctrine. This Satanic philosophy mistakenly holds that if one surrenders his will to the will of God, then that one would become a mere automaton, devoid of any self-awareness. But the exact opposite is in fact true. Through willfully uniting with God, one attains the supreme self-realization. In order to understand this, it is first necessary to understand the divisions of Man, i.e. the hylic, or physical; the psychic, or soul; and the pneumatic, or spiritual. When we speak of salvation, or divinization, we are really talking about the spiritualization of the soul. The pneumatic essence in Man is that pure, uncreated light. But only that which is pneumatic can behold the pneumatic. It is therefore through the gradual purification of the soul - the spiritualization of the psychic substance - that the pneumatic is realized, and that regeneration and reintegration can occur.

Amazingly, though, there is at least one fairly well-known so-called Christian Gnostic church that adheres to the childish and unenlightened Setian/Satanic philosophy. It is childish because it is based on the primal childhood fear of the dark, of death, of non-being. It is unenlightened because every true student of the Mysteries knows that to be initiated is to learn how to die. Those who yet hold to this fear have not yet received the Wisdom of initiation. This doctrine of the unenlightened is lacking because it stagnates at the rational, unable to grasp the trans-rational, or mystical. The church I have referred to, which shall remain unnamed, seems in its outer manifestations to adhere to the ancient and traditional doctrines of the gnosis. But within the teachings of the highest level of its inner order are found the erroneous doctrines we have mentioned. I know this to be true because I myself was admitted into its highest ranks and served for a time in an administrative position. While I will not quote directly from the documents of this church, you can find the general doctrine discussed throughout Stephen Flowers' Lords of the Left-Hand Path.

This idea of possibly losing one's identity is terrifying not only to Satanists and Setian-derived Gnostic churches, but to the Roman Catholic church as well. There has long been an aversion in the West to the mysticism of the Eastern church. And even though Catholicism has been slowly warming up to the Eastern doctrines and practices, the cloud of rational scholasticism still looms large. While the Eastern Orthodox church fears the heresy of apotheosis, the Catholic fears tend toward the other direction. A recent article in the Catholic magazine "Inside the Vatican" states:

> The true Christian understanding of *Theosis* rejects any form of pantheism and any idea that all individuals cease, becoming fused into one single identity, or swallowed up (as some Eastern religions hold) into the deity. Rather, the individual remains a person in integrity, in fact, truly becoming [the] person [he] is created to be.

This sounds suspiciously similar to the Satanic philosophy previously mentioned, and is tending toward a view that is inconsistent with the experience of mystics throughout history. As Gnostics, theosis consists of the reintegration of the Pleroma, as explained in Ambelain's Spiritual Alchemy:

> *Reintegration,* or the reconstitution of the pleroma,
> consists of the slow and progressive working out of
> the Preexistent Church dispersed by the Fall. Now,
> this Church is the Mystic Body of Christ.

This concept of the reuniting of the divine fragments dispersed by the Fall is central to both ancient and modern Gnostic theology. While Gnosticism may not hold much in the way of dogma, there are nevertheless a number of doctrines which are held almost universally. Reintegration into the divine Fullness is one such doctrine. It is therefore our opinion that the Gnostic character of any individual or church who expounds a doctrine contrary to this traditional teaching must be considered suspect at least.

In summary, we can say that the Orthodox doctrine of theosis may be shared in almost every respect by the Gnostic. The practical methods of attaining illumination and theosis - asceticism and sacramental participation - are substantially the same for the Orthodox and the Gnostic. Gnosticism's doctrine of emanation, however, allows for the natural immanence of God, which is validated through the genuine mystical experience. Orthodox doctrine suffers in part from having to try to reconcile the mystical experience with codified dogma. The Orthodox, therefore, must create complicated definitions and clever word play in order to justify the undeniable experience of the mystics while escaping the label of "heretic" - i.e. Gnostic, Bogomil, etc. The Gnostic merely states plainly what is understood by the mystic who has attained to the Vision. To be sure, the Gnostic is not without a set of relatively complicated doctrines and definitions, but there is no need for him to rationalize his experience in a way that is not seen to violate dogma.

It is only because of the immanence of divinity that we are able to participate fully in the divine nature. For divinization represents a sort of spiritual evolution. And nothing can *evolve* which was not already *involved*. This process of spiritual evolution is effected through gnosis, by which the veils of obscurity may be lifted, revealing the divine inner light. And it is through this immanent light that we are connected to the unknowable and transcendent Father. I would encourage all of our Gnostic brothers and sisters to thoroughly acquaint themselves with the doctrines and practices of theosis, including the Hesychastic method. Even though the ancient Gnostics were suppressed long ago, the gnosis itself can never be extinguished. We can learn much from our Orthodox brethren, and even those in the Roman church who have developed such worthy methods as the *lectio divina* system of contemplative scripture reading. By learning about and utilizing those ideas and methods which are good from Orthodox and Catholic sources, we will do much to further the Great Work of the reintegration of the Preexistent Church.